Country Wisdom

Timeless Values and Virtues from the American Heartland

Jerry Apps

Voyageur Press

Previously published as *Rural Wisdom* by Amherst Press

Cover design by Julie Vermeer
Printed in China

05 06 07 08 09 5 4 3 2 1

Library of Congress Cataloging-in-Publication Data

Apps, Jerold W., 1934-
[Rural wisdom]
Country wisdom : timeless values and virtues from the American heartland / Jerry Apps.
p. cm.
Previously published as: Rural wisdom. 1997.
ISBN 0-89658-718-5 (pbk. : alk. paper)
1. Country life--Middle West--Quotations, maxims, etc. 2. Country life--Middle West--Anecdotes. 3. Middle West--Social life and customs--Quotations, maxims, etc. 4. Middle West--Social life and customs--Anecdotes. 5. Conduct of life--Quotations, maxims, etc. 6. Conduct of life--Anecdotes. I. Title.
F351.A67 2005
977--dc22
2005004846

Published by Voyageur Press, Inc.
123 North Second Street, P.O. Box 338, Stillwater, MN 55082 U.S.A.
651-430-2210, fax 651-430-2211
books@voyageurpress.com
www.voyageurpress.com

Dedication

To my father, Herman Apps ...
who was a farmer, storyteller, and an encyclopedia of rural wisdom.

Cover photo is Herman Apps, father of the author, Jerry Apps. The back cover shows Jerry with his grandson. All photographs taken by Steve Apps, son of Jerry, grandson of Herman and uncle of Josh.

Contents

Preface

Ask a person brought up in the country to say something wise and you'll get a strange look. Rural people don't run around spouting words of wisdom. On the other hand, once you get to know them they'll tell you story after story about their lives and the people they know. The wisdom is there, in these stories and comments.

Having grown up on a Wisconsin farm, I heard these stories as long as I can remember. My father and my grandfather were storytellers. So were my uncles. And so were several of the neighbors in our Waushara County community located some four miles west of Wild Rose, Wisconsin. I heard stories whenever the family gathered. I also heard them when neighbors got together to share work projects. In 1966, I acquired my own farm, where I live part-time, discovering something new and recalling something old almost every day.

When my 93-year-old father died a few years ago, I began writing down some of his sayings I remembered from my growing up years on the farm. Soon I began recalling *wisdom* that I had gathered from other rural people that I met over the years.

I am indebted to many people for the ideas in this book, especially my father. I also want to thank my three children for taking time in their busy lives to read this material and offer suggestions for improvement. My daughter Susan, an elementary school teacher in Madison, has an eye for what makes sensible prose. Jeff, a hotel sales manager in Colorado, raises practical questions. Steve, the journalist in the family and staff photographer for the *Wisconsin State Journal* in Madison, reads with an eye for interest and understanding. Steve also did the photography for the book. Ruth, my wife and live-in editor, read unending drafts of the book, challenging, but always supporting. Finally, the staff of Amherst Press and especially Charles and Roberta Spanbauer have supported my work and encouraged topics that range from one-room country schools to rural wisdom. To all of these people and many more, I am indebted. Their wisdom has helped to make the wisdom of this book more accessible, and I hope, both interesting and valuable.

Jerry Apps

APPLE
EMPORIUM
OPEN

1

Rural Wisdom

When I graduated eighth grade from a Wisconsin one-room country school, I looked forward to attending high school in Wild Rose, some four miles from our farm. I suspect it was during the first few weeks in high school that I discovered, firsthand, the differences between city kids and country kids. We country kids learned quickly that we were supposedly inferior to the more sophisticated high school freshmen who had grown up in town. At least that is what we heard from our new "town friends" who attended classes with us.

Even the teachers contributed to our feelings of inferiority, although I don't think they did it intentionally. We were encouraged to put behind us our "country ways" and learn how the world really worked; that the only people who really made a difference were city people, and that country folk were backwater hicks who had few social skills and had a lot to learn before they could make it in the world.

When I left the farm to attend the University in Madison, I faced the country-city difference again. Only this time I was smarter. I vowed that I could act "city" and that no one need know that I grew up on a sandy farm in Waushara County, Wisconsin, where our farmhouse didn't have electricity until I was a sophomore in high school, and had no indoor plumbing until several years after I left home. I remember so well my first day at the University. My new roommate was from Rockford, Illinois. "Jerry," he said, "you walk like you're behind a plow." I didn't respond. The truth was that I had been walking behind a plow only a few days earlier, but I wasn't about to tell my new roommate that he had been stuck with a country hick. I learned how to walk "city."

As the years flew by, I graduated from college, spent some time in the army, and then returned to Wisconsin to work as a county extension agent. I immediately felt at home working with rural people, I also discovered that I had learned some things as a farm kid that my city friends didn't know, and that these things turned out to be extremely important to me as I changed jobs and raised a family. Some of what I knew was practical farm kid stuff, like knowing when to plant corn, how to help a cow give birth, and telling the difference between a heifer, a steer, a bull, and a cow. I am constantly surprised at people who see an animal in a field and call it a cow, even when it is a steer, and sometimes even a bull.

I'd learned other things that were not so tangible. Growing up on a farm we learned how to work, how to cooperate with others, and the importance of our neighbors. We learned about nature that was so much a part of our lives, about the land and how we depended on it, and about the weather and how it affected us.

Imbedded in who I am is a set of beliefs and values that guide what I do, how I see the world, and how I relate to other people. These beliefs and values came out of my rural upbringing, and no matter how much I had at one time wanted to ignore them, they are still there. These beliefs and values were always important to me, even when I didn't know it.

The topics in this book range over what people in the Midwest have thought and experienced. There is advice about what to wear, what to eat, how to grow a garden, and directions for making sauerkraut. There are comments about the weather, about work, and about the seasons, particularly winter. Family is a theme, so is the family farm. What to do when you get a cold (spread skunk grease on your chest, prepare a whiskey sling, and go to bed early) is here. So is advice about bathing too often. Although some of the ideas are rooted in history, many have application today. The statements are both serious and light, with some tongue-in-cheek. Many have meanings that go deeper than the words, just as what you see on the surface of the land is only a sampling of what is really there.

You need not live in the country to see yourself on these pages. These statements have application that cut across time and place.

2

Making a Living

Work always defined rural life, yesterday as well as today. On midwestern farms, the work day begins at an early hour, during much of the year before the sun rises, and continues into the evening when the livestock are fed and the evening chores are done.

It is easy to conclude that a rural person's life is one of drudgery. For some it is, but for most, work is enjoyed, nearly all the time anyway. Some tasks are enjoyed more than others. No one that I knew enjoyed hoeing potatoes hour after hour under a hot June sun, or walking behind a team of horses pulling a drag that lifted clouds of dust so thick you could scarcely see the horses heads in front of you.

But other tasks made up for the less desirable ones. Going after the cows on a dewy morning in spring with bird song everywhere and the sun edging over the horizon was one of them. Hauling hay into an old empty barn, with the sweet smells of drying hay, and the satisfaction of seeing the haymows filled to the rafters was another.

Rural people are popularly thought of as rugged indivdualists, preferring to work alone. True, many tasks on the farm are done alone. But over the years, many jobs required cooperation with neighbors working together. Threshing grain was a community affair, with farmers all working together and moving from farm to farm in the neighborhood until everyone's grain was in the granary. Silo filling, corn shredding and wood sawing were also community tasks during the years before forage harvesters, corn combines, and oil heating.

Of course these community work projects were much more than work; they were social activities. As neighbors worked together, they talked about everything from their crops to the weather and the price of milk. When it was mealtime, the work stopped and the everyone ate together at the host's house. It was a time of storytelling and laughter, of sharing and caring, although these words were never used. These neighborhood work projects helped tie rural communities together, to give them a oneness, and an identity.

Rural people take great pride in their work. It doesn't matter if the task is picking cucumbers, building a barn or making a fence. The job is done well, to the best of the person's ability. Barn builders were a good example of this. When they finished a barn, they brought friends and relatives to see it. For these barn builders, each new barn was a part of who they were, what they believed, and of course their craftsmanship.

Getting Things Done

Begin each day with the difficult things. Thinking about the easier things to come makes the time fly.

Do the work that requires thought when you are fresh.

A task started is half completed. Picking up hay bales in a twenty-acre field is an example. The task looks impossible until the first couple of bales are on the wagon.

Doing work with immediate result, such as splitting wood or painting a fence, helps cushion the times when work shows little gain such as teaching a new calf to drink out of a pail or discussing politics with your brother-in-law.

Asking the right question is two-thirds of the way toward its answer.

Clear thoughts lead to clear action. Muddled thoughts lead to muddled action.

Work

Let your deeds tell your story. Don't blow your horn too loudly, just enough so people won't run over you.

It is better to wear out than rust out.

Who you are is more important than what you have accomplished.

With a little more effort, what was done well could have been exceptional. We often stop too soon. We are willing to accept "good enough" without striving for something special. When you believe that you've done the best job possible, consider that the beginning place for doing something outstanding.

When you work for someone else, always do more than what is asked. Come to work earlier than required and stay a little later.

Exchange work with a neighbor, but don't worry about exchanging money. If your neighbor helps you for a half day, expect to help him a half day. It doesn't matter the task. Don't worry if you believe a half day of chopping wood is worth more than a half day of unloading hay bales. In the end it will all work out, and you will continue having good neighbors.

Try to do more for others than they do for you.

Learn how to work well with others; learn how to work well alone.

Worrying that your neighbor is achieving more than you are prevents you from doing your best.

Many people are more capable than you, and, likewise, many are less capable. Just do your best and don't worry about others.

Striving for perfection may prevent you from doing your best work.

We all can do better than we think we can.

Work is never done, so take time to play.

Work isn't nearly as important as most people would make it.

To take work too seriously often takes the fun out of the rest of life.

If thoughts of your work consistently awaken you in the dark hours of the night, look for other work.

Using your head when you work often results in less use of your hands.

Do you want your tombstone to read, "All he did was work"? How many of us lead our lives as if that were the case?

Better to risk going hungry than to continue on a job you don't like.

Recognize that there is good and bad in every job. The idea is to find work that is more agreeable than disagreeable.

An enjoyable job for one person may be another person's torment.

Working too hard for too long a time is often harmful. A heavy rain does not continue for an entire day, nor does a deer run without stopping to rest.

Succeeding in work usually means working day after day, year after year, but it also means finding time for fun and family life.

Machines

Machines can teach us much, if we give them a chance, especially do they teach patience and tolerance.

Make sure that you control your machines, and that they do not control you.

OilPull
TRACTOR
ROCK ISLAND
435
DIESEL

Keep your tools and machinery well oiled and in good repair. An hour spent oiling can prevent three hours of fixing.

The bigger and more expensive machine you buy, whether it's a tractor, a plow or a corn combine, doesn't always mean more money in your pocket. It often means no money in your pants at all; sometimes you even lose your pants.

Thinking and Doing

Take time to think in the middle of doing. A few minutes thinking can save hours of doing.

Doing without thinking is dangerous; thinking without doing is misguided.

Sometimes we must do and think at the same time.

To be caught thinking while not doing is to be labeled lazy. Invent excuses for thinking:

- Break for a drink of water.
- Swab your kerchief across your sweaty brow.
- Ask for time to catch your breath.

Extended periods of thinking require grandeur excuses:

- Go fishing.
- Hike out to check the crops.
- Wash the windows in the barn.
- Split a pile of wood.
- Wash a sink full of dishes.

Some men work so slow you have to set up a stick to see if they are moving.

George Miller had a willing pair of sons. One was willing to work and the other was willing to let him.

Money

- It is no disgrace to be poor, just rather inconvenient at times.

- Save as much money as you can, but watch where you put it. The bank closings of the Depression years provide powerful memories for not taking any savings place for granted.

- Money and happiness don't agree.

- If you don't have the money to buy something, hold off buying until you do. The exception is buying land.

- Even when your income is small, put some money away. You never know when your income will be smaller still, or disappear altogether.

- Never let money come between you and a friend. Better to give a friend some money than lend it.

- Living to accumulate money is not living.

- One man's wealth is another man's poverty.

- Money can't buy your health, a sunset, a friendship, or a baby's laughter.

- Pay your bills on time, a little early if possible.

- To worry about money is to take your mind away from important matters.

- No matter how much money we have, we all grow old and die.

- Friendship can't be purchased.

- The farmer who paints his barn with more expensive white paint wants his neighbors with red barns to know he has more money than they do. The color of a barn's paint doesn't matter. What makes a difference is the quality of its roof and the sturdiness of its foundation.

"Marry for money and love will come" is advice sometimes heard. Unfortunately, those who heed the suggestion usually acquire neither.

Many people become slaves to their possessions.

3

Farming

Farmers are the heart and soul of the country. In the settlement years of the Midwest, more people worked as farmers than any other occupation. As the years passed, farmers began leaving the land, with now less than two percent of the U.S. population farming.

The values and beliefs held by farmers who settled the region, and the children and grandchildren that followed them on the land, forged the basic foundation for today's midwestern people. Some modern-day folks say farmers and farm life are historic relics, replaced by high-tech modern day agriculturists who farm hundreds, sometimes thousands, of acres and milk as many cows. Those who say this know little about farmers and farming.

Family farmers, from those who worked the soil during pioneer days to the present time, are a special people. Famed Tuskegee educator Booker T. Washington, in 1895, wrote, "No race can prosper till it learns there is as much dignity in tilling a field as in writing a poem." That advice still holds.

Here is a sprinkling of farm wisdom:

- Anyone can farm, but not everyone is a farmer.
- Farming is like playing five-card poker with four cards.
- Farmers never have good years, only some years that are less bad than others.
- Farmers produce food, not products. Products come from factories; food comes from the land.

- No one understands the land as well as farmers, for the land not only supports them but nurtures their souls.

- Farming is more than *making* a living. It is *about* living and the connection of people to the earth.

- No machine can replace the eye of the farmer in caring for animals, producing crops, or appreciating the land.

- There is reason to suspect the sanity of a farmer who does not complain.

- Successful farmers know the beliefs and values that made their parents successful, and they try to follow them.

- Successful farming has more to do with values such as hard work, cooperation with neighbors, frugality, caring for the environment, and common sense than with science and technology.

- Today, many farmers produce more to earn less.

- The history of the land is etched in the faces of the farmers who till it.

- For a farmer, next year will always be better.

- The family farm is a model for farming *and* a model for family. Often three generations work and live together—older sharing wisdom with younger, younger sharing enthusiasm with older.

- Bigger is not better when it comes to farm size. Ability to care for the land ought be a guide, not whether a person can negotiate a loan to buy more.

- Attending to details makes all the difference, whether it's plowing a field, building a fence, or teaching a newborn calf to drink.

When a farm is sold, for whatever reason, a part of the family is sold as well. Farmers who live and work the land cannot easily sell and move to the city. Too many emotions are involved, and too much history. Usually several generations have grown up and worked the same acreage. To sever a relationship with the land is like losing a child. It is more difficult than words can express.

Milking Cows

There is no better way to understand animals than to milk cows twice a day, every day.

Cows expect the same fair treatment, day after day, no matter how you feel, or what has happened to you before you enter the barn. Good advice when working with people as well.

Milking cows is a wonderful time for thinking, about everything from what you plan to do when you grow older to the meaning of what you did last night.

Milking cows teaches patience. Milking can't be hurried much. If you try to hurry you likely get a tail across your face, or a cow's foot planted on your boot.

Milking cows with your parents is a wonderful time to discuss those things with your father or mother that take time. There is plenty of time when the cows are milked, time for thoughts to settle in and move around in your mind before they are responded to.

Milking cows is a time to warm up after a cold day cutting wood when the temperature is below zero.

Learning to know another living creature is never at a higher level than when you are milking a cow.

When milking cows, you learn about individual differences and how they must be attended to. Some cows milk easy, some hard. Some have skittish personalities and jump at the least distraction such as when a barn cat races in front of them. Others are docile and wouldn't move if the barn were falling down. Some like to be milked and let you know it by lowing softly. A few despise you and let you know it by kicking at you, trying to dump your milk pail, or slapping you in the face with their tails. Yet, in all instances, you make adjustments and keep on milking.

Threshing

In my home community in central Wisconsin, threshing season rolled around in late summer, when the oat, wheat, and rye crop was ripe, and the grain had been cut with a binder, the bundles placed in shocks and then allowed to dry for a few days. Much wisdom came from threshing season, now only a memory for many farmers since combines have replaced the threshing machine.

When it's time to thresh, it is time to thresh. Nothing is more important. When a neighbor says the threshing machine is coming to the community, prepare to spend up to a couple weeks threshing, helping out your neighbors as they will help you when the threshing machine comes to your farm.

Threshing is that time of year when you can check all of the neighbors' cooking. Some are great cooks, and you try to adjust the threshing progress to make sure that you can eat as many meals at their places as possible. A few are terrible cooks. You thresh and leave as quickly as possible, trying to avoid all meals, but usually having to suffer through at least one.

If it's your job to pitch bundles into the ever-hungry threshing machine, and you are growing tired, toss a few bundles in crosswise. The machine will growl and groan and plug, causing the man in charge to shut down the machine to clean it. You have gained a rest. But be careful; the man in charge knows what you have done and you are likely to get away with it only once.

When you have a choice, try to drive a bundle wagon. This means you haul bundles from the field, and have a little time to rest while you travel to and from the field and the threshing machine. It's also much cooler out in the grain field where the breezes blow. Around the threshing machine and the farm buildings it is much hotter.

Building a straw stack is probably the worst job of all those associated with threshing because you sink into the fresh straw up to your waist, the distributor pipe blows straw on top of you, and someone is always yelling for you to stack a little more straw here, or a little more there.

The second worst job is shoveling freshly threshed oats in the granary. The carriers, the men toting the grain in bags from the machine to the granary, empty the heavy canvas bags in the front of the grain bin. Your job is to shovel the grain to the back of the bin. A job for someone too young to drive a bundle wagon, but no job for anyone who can't tolerate dust. Grain bins are filled with dust, and they are hot, and the work is never-ending. Sometimes building a straw stack is a pleasant break from shoveling grain in a bin.

When the day's threshing is done, it is a good time to enjoy a bottle of cold beer: usually a favorite of the farmer where you are threshing. Everyone had his favorite beer: Berliner, Chief Oshkosh, Point Special, Miller High Life, Blatz, Schlitz, Pabst, Heileman's, and several others. Great arguments developed over which was the best beer. The arguments, in good fun, went on from farm to farm and they were never settled. But the beer, no matter what its label, was always enjoyed.

Plowing

- The worth of a man is measured by how straight he can plow.

- More so than the calendar, plowing marks the beginning of the year, the start of the growing season.

- A farmer is never closer to the land than when he is plowing.

- No smell is sweeter, more looked forward to each year, than that of freshly turned soil.

- Like the artist who paints a canvas with a brush, a farmer paints the landscape with a plow, creating ribbons of black and brown.

Barns

- If it's a choice between putting a new roof on the barn or on your house, choose the barn. If your farm animals are uncomfortable, you may soon not have a barn or a house roof to replace.

- Barns are agricultural history in red paint.

- There is no orchestra that can surpass the sound of rain on a barn roof.

- A barn is like a cathedral, a vast expanse of space holding back the elements, and connecting people to a larger power.

- Tear down an old barn and destroy a piece of your heritage.

- Stand inside an empty barn on a windy day; listen to it complain as the wind whistles around the corners and rattles the hinges on the doors.

- Enjoy the warmth of a cow barn on a cold day in winter. It is a natural warmth created by the animals housed there, and different from the artificial heat that warms your home.

Land

- The land is a mystery. It constantly surprises, and sometimes disappoints. But it is always the land.

- When we treat the land like a machine, measuring it and testing it, forming it and shaping it, it often rebels. The land is reminding us that it, too, lives. None of us wants to be treated like a machine. Neither does the land.

- The land is soil, but more. Land is never dirt. Dirt is what accumulates behind the refrigerator, and what we track into the kitchen on our shoes.

- The land is always changing, but remaining changeless.

- When we own land it also owns us.

- Owning land is a great responsibility, for we really can't own it. We are only stewards for a time as the land moves from owner to owner.

- A foundation for human ethics is developing an ethic toward the land.

- How people care for the land today is an indicator of whether they will have something to eat tomorrow.

- How a person treats the land is a window onto how a person treats other people.

- The extent to which we sever our connections with the land is the extent to which we disconnect ourselves from our souls.

Stones

- Stones in the fields of many sizes and hues—red, brown, gray, black. In the way. Despised. Cursed.

- Stones off the fields of many shapes and colors—into building barns and churches and schools. Useful. Beautiful. Praised.

Working in a stony field, like life, requires you to be constantly alert. You never know when you'll come up against a hard-headed stone that you didn't see. Failing to act quickly can mean a broken plow point, a twisted cultivator shovel, or a dulled sickle bar in your mower.

4

Practical Matters

When you live five miles from town you learn how to fix things for yourself, a broken farm implement, a leaking pipe, even a sick animal. And you learn how to do things in the most practical way possible because you don't have time or money to take the long way around for doing something.

Suggestions

- Carry a jackknife. One blade should have enough edge so you can sharpen a pencil or do a little whittling. The other blade is best left dull. Use the dull blade for scraping grease off machinery, slitting open your mail, or in a pinch, serving as a screwdriver.

- In another pocket carry a pair of pliers. With a jackknife and pliers you can make assorted repairs and work yourself out of many difficulties. A pair of pliers can do everything from cutting wire to pounding in a staple on a fence where the wire has popped loose.

- Good idea to carry a few eight-penny nails in your pocket as well. There is always a loose board that needs fixing. You can even use a nail as a staple, to fasten wire to a fence post. Just drive it in part way, and bend it over. Not a pretty sight, but it works.

- Carry a pocket watch. Used to be that you could buy a good Pocket Ben for $1.00; that was the case for many years. They cost more now, but serve as well. A watch on your wrist is always in trouble. When you are splitting wood you shake the bejeebers out of it, sometimes even shaking off the hands. Nothing worse than a watch that keeps good time but can't tell anyone. A pocket watch is always there, ticking away. Of course you have to fish for it to find out the time, but there's no reason to look at your watch more than a couple times a day anyway—at dinner time and at supper time. Grandchildren like pocket watches, too. They put the watch to their ear and listen to the "tick-tock." One of Grandpa's many mysteries.

- Keep the chimneys on your lamps clean. A smoky chimney blocks out at least half the lamp's light.

- Learn to fix things yourself. You have both the satisfaction of doing it your way, and the knowledge that you've saved some money.

- Know when to ask someone else to fix something for you. What is broken a little may be broken a lot when you start fixing it.

- Keep things simple. They'll get complicated enough, soon enough, without you intending that they should.

- Estimate the amount of time you believe it will take to complete a task. Then double it. Almost everything takes longer than you think it will, a lot longer.

- Try new ideas, but go slow. Let a new idea roll around in your head for a couple of weeks before acting on it, maybe even longer.

- If you need to measure something and you don't have a ruler, use a dollar bill—it's a shade over six inches long.

- To gauge distance, measure your stride; for many people it is about a yard. Then walk, count your steps and you have a rough estimate of the number of yards. Rural people call it "pacing off a distance." Measure twice, cut once. Good advice for a lot more than just carpentry.

When you are furious with someone, hold your tongue. When you get home, write the person a letter, venting all your anger. Burn the letter.

Clothing

Wear simple clothing. A cotton shirt and a couple pair of bib overalls are about all a man needs, except for going to church. New overalls for trips to town on Saturday night. Faded overalls for work.

A woman needs several good aprons, the kind that come up to the neck and extend below a dress, and have a couple of pockets to carry a few safety pins and a handkerchief. A good apron protects a dress from spills and splashes, and it's a convenient place to dry your hands, gather eggs, wipe away a child's tears, and wave when you want Joe's attention out in the back forty.

Never buy a shirt that doesn't have a pocket. You need the pocket for a small notebook and a pencil.

Always wear long sleeved shirts. They protect from mosquitoes and other pests, prevent excessive sunburn, and can be rolled up when the weather is warm. Short sleeved shirts have no such multiple use.

Avoid wearing a necktie; it cuts off circulation to the brain and thus prevents clear thinking.

Don't wear pants with a belt; the tightness around the stomach prevents good digestion.

Never wear short pants. They were made for people who never walk through a wild raspberry patch, or knee-high wet grass.

Don't go outside without your shirt. If God had meant for you to run around naked, you would have been born that way.

Wear a straw hat in summer, and a wool cap with ear flaps in winter. When your head is cool, your body is cool; when your head is warm, your body is warm. It's as simple as that.

5

Lifetime Learning

Everyone must keep learning; rural people have long known this. Every new piece of machinery, every new crop variety, every planting season, requires new learning. Stories abound about farmers who bought their first tractors after driving horses for years. To stop a horse, you say, "whoa." Most of the time it will stop. Yelling "whoa" to a tractor is akin to yelling "stop" when the wind is blowing. Nothing happens. The tractor smashes through the end of the new tractor shed. Learning to operate a tractor thus required first some unlearning.

Rural people had various ways of describing a person's ability to learn, or lack of it. "He's a little slow." "She's sharper than a tack." "She's wiser than a tree full of owls." "He's dumber than a stump." "The barn's there but the haymow's empty."

Learning

- What we already know can prevent us from learning something new. We must first learn how to rid ourselves of old ideas and ways of doing things. We must also develop the wisdom to know what to discard and what to keep, for old ideas and old ways may be better than those that are new.

- Understand as much as you can, about as many things as you are able, but realize there are mysteries that cannot be understood—why a prize-winning cow dies unexpectedly, or why some summers it rains and the crops grow thick and tall, and other summers it is so dry the cows must be fed hay by mid-July.

- Our need and ability to take things apart and name each piece prevents us from seeing wholes, from seeing what something really is, rather than just knowing the pieces that comprise it. A tree is more than its trunk, branches, roots and leaves.

- To understand a forest, we must know more than the trees.

- Knowing your weakness is the first step toward strength.

- We are often obsessed with accumulating answers for which there are no questions.

- Find those who are wise and follow them.

- Knowing is more than collecting information. Many people are informed, few know.

- Learn to figure in your head. You will often have the answers before someone with a fancy figuring machine.

- Be careful of people who seem to have all the answers—professors, preachers, politicians, and relatives. Listen politely, but then make up your own mind.

- The world is full of people who can find fault with ideas. Those who create new ideas are few in number.

- You can learn in many ways. Working at a job you don't know how to do, talking with a person you've never met, traveling to a place you've never been, eating a food you've never tasted, or walking a trail you've never hiked can provide wonderful learning opportunities.

- Never stop reading. Read books, all kinds of books, fact and fiction, usual and unusual, and ordinary books written by local people with a story to tell and a message to share.

- We often learn much when we least expect to: the loss of a favorite dog, the death of a parent, when a hailstorm destroys our corn crop, the birth of a child.

- A rope is weakest at the place it is knotted. Our lives, too, are most vulnerable at the place of our knots—our unchanging perspectives, our rigid beliefs, our outdated approaches. It is when we untie our knots that we can become strong again. Untying a knot is one form of learning.

- "What will other people think?" prevents many of us from following our interests, exploring our dreams, learning what most do not learn, or even consider learning.

- Our teachers are many if we will recognize them as such: our children and their questions, a thunderstorm and its power, a flock of Canada geese and their cooperation, a soaring eagle and its freedom, the promise that comes with spring, and the love between a baby and its mother.

If we try to learn too quickly, we will often miss the understanding that time and contemplation provide.

Teaching

- All of us teach, whether we intend to or not.

- We teach by who we are and what we do, much more so than by what we say.

- Teaching is sharing and caring, listening and watching, questioning and answering, receiving and giving.

- A good teacher is one who helps students become their own teachers.

- To learn a subject well, try to teach it to someone else.

- Classrooms are everywhere, not merely rooms with four walls and desks in rows. Good teachers know this well. The country is a classroom without comparison.

Telling a story is a powerful teaching approach. Good storytellers are important teachers, even though they may not think of themselves as such.

New and Old Ideas

- To walk eighty rods on a never before traveled trail is far more difficult than traveling five miles on a well-used road.

- Any new idea is suspect and subject to ridicule.

- New ideas are like tiny oaks; they need time to become established and push forth their leaves. Like the tiny oak, new ideas are often chewed off or smashed flat before they are recognized for what they are.

- Support a person with a new idea. It may appear foolish, or not workable, different from anything you've heard before. Give it a chance. If we never accepted a new idea, we'd still be living in caves, looking forward to the discovery of fire.

- Avoid making fun of your neighbor who tries something new: a new variety of corn, a different way of making hay, a new kind of wire fence. You will avoid embarrassing yourself when you discover the neighbor has something that you would like to try.

- Avoid criticizing your neighbor who insists on doing things the old way. New ways are not always better ways.

- Take some time to figure out what of the old you want to keep, and what new ideas you want to follow. Caring about people is an old idea; buying a big new tractor is a new idea.

- Do not equate new with big. Many people have confused these words. Avoid mixing up big with better, and, likewise, new with better. Big is often worse, so is new.

- What is worth more, a new idea or many repetitions of any old idea?

- New ideas often emerge from old ideas by giving them a new twist. The upright silo resulted when someone decided to stand a horizontal silo on end.

6

Family

Families have been central to rural life from the time when the first settlers arrived in the Midwest to the present time. Early farms, and most farms today, are family enterprises. The entire family works together, everyone with a task and a responsibility, from the youngest to the oldest. On the farm where I grew up, the first job, when you were four or five years old, was to fill the ever-empty wood box in the kitchen. As you got older, you graduated to feeding the chickens and gathering eggs—assuming that you had younger brothers and sisters to take over what was previously your responsibility. From the chickens, you moved to the barn, to help with the barn chores, first feeding the calves, then milking cows, forking hay from the haymow, and shoveling manure.

These latter chores were of the highest order; you looked forward to doing them. Once your father determined you were ready, you did the task to the very best of your ability. You not only learned how to do the work—learning how to milk a cow by hand took a little learning, forking hay was no great challenge, neither was shoveling manure—you did it without complaining.

These were family responsibilities. If you didn't do your chores, then someone else in the family had to do them. Sometimes you traded jobs. You fed the chickens for your brother so he could spend time with a school friend. Trading jobs was OK, as long as the work got done, and was done right.

Our father was a stickler for doing jobs right. We never could quite do the jobs well enough, and occasionally he reminded us of this fact. But he accepted our trying to improve, to do the task in the best possible way.

Of course, as a family, we did things besides work. We drove to town on Saturday nights so my mother could grocery shop. We went fishing in Norwegian Lake. We swam in Chain O' Lakes. We drove to Adams County in late summer and picked blueberries. All of these were family activities.

Our closest neighbors lived more than a half mile away. We were, in some respects, isolated, and only had each other. Our isolation brought us together as a family. So did knowing that the very success of our farm depended on each of us doing our share and making our contribution to the overall effort. Some of what I have learned about family follows:

- Families that work together learn the meaning of cooperation and respect. There are no pretenses during haying season, when each member of the family has a job to do, and each depends on the other. This principle holds for almost all other tasks that rural families face.

- Family comes first, before work, ahead of play, beyond everything else that may look so important at the time.

- Little things keep a marriage alive, a word of praise, an unexpected gift, a trip to the city for dinner.

- Being kind is more important than being perfect.

- Hugs speak of caring. Hug your spouse, often.

- Trust is key in keeping a family together and a marriage alive.

- Always sit down and talk through a disagreement rather than letting it fester unresolved. But wait a little before you talk, to allow the anger to disappear and the emotions to calm.

- Love is a hard word for many rural people to say. Spouses like to hear it from each other, at least once a day, even when the excuse is, "She (or he) knows it, why must I say it?"

Children

- The two most important things we can give our children are roots as deep as a giant oak's, and wings as strong as an eagle's.

- Help your children see the importance of their name, and how once it is tarnished it will remain so, no matter how hard they work to make it otherwise.

- Children who do not see love at home will have difficulty seeing it anywhere else.

- Allow your children to be children. The childhood years are few; the adult years are many. Having chores to do is important; so is having time to play.

- What a child learns at home will remain forever.

- There is no such thing as hugging a child too much.

- Show children, don't tell them. Show them the meaning of honesty, of caring and sharing, and concern for those who have less than you do—through your actions.

- When a child asks "why?" take time to answer, no matter how often the question is repeated.

- Allow your children to grow up being who they are, not who you want them to be. Even if you try to do this, who you are will be reflected in the words and actions of your children.

- Your children can be your best teachers, especially in helping you become aware of what you take for granted: "Why is the sky blue?" "Where do eggs come from?" "Where does the sun go at night?" "Why does it thunder?"

No matter how much you might think otherwise, you are your children's most important teacher.

Grandchildren are wonderful reminders of the things you forgot about your own children, or were too busy raising them to notice.

Talk to little children, listen to them for their ideas are fresh. Watch them. Learn from them. They are real and experiencing life to the fullest.

A sleepy child is a good child. Children with jobs to do don't have time to get into trouble, or the energy.

There is no better discipline than hoeing thistles in a corn field for eight hours, under a hot July sun. Something valuable is accomplished, too.

Support your children's teacher. You and she (he) are a team. You need each other, but more importantly, your child needs parents and teachers working together.

Children may ignore your advice, but they will never ignore your example. They notice how you treat animals, how you care for the crops, what you say about your neighbor, and what you think of rural life.

7

For Good Health

There is lots of wisdom about health in the Midwest. Much of it is practical, down to earth and good advice today as it was a hundred years ago, when doctors were scarce and a hospital was a day's trip or more away. Some of it may have had value in an earlier day, but is not something anyone would recommend now. For instance, filling a pillow with hops instead of feathers in order to sleep better. Some of the advice was silly, yet people swore by a particular practice's effectiveness. My grandmother insisted that when you had a fever, you went to bed and piled on the covers. The idea was to sweat out the fever. Some of the old treatments, such as drinking worm root tea to calm an upset stomach, worked because of the natural ingredients present in the plant.

I don't recall anyone ever using words like "mental health" and "depression" when I was growing up. People said things like "down in the dumps," "feeling blue," and "moody" to describe a woman's mental state. For men, the words were more likely "Something wrong with Joe, he's not right these days," or "Ben's sure got ornery since his best cow died."

We knew that health was more than what happened to the body, and we had advice on what to do about it. Here are some healthful suggestions:

For Good Health

- Go to bed early; get up early. The best hours of the day are before noon. The best hours of all are before breakfast.

- When you develop a bad cold, ease the symptoms by drinking a whiskey sling. Make a whiskey sling by pouring a shot of whiskey into a glass of hot water, and adding a little lemon to help make the concoction go down easier. Repeat if necessary.

If your chest is congested, rub on an ample amount of skunk grease. Pin a square of flannel to your underwear to keep the power of the skunk grease in rather than moving out. To dispel any disbelief, skunk grease bears none of the interesting aroma associated with its source. It has no smell whatever.

Always keep a supply of skunk grease handy. In addition to its medicinal qualities, it makes a wonderful preservative for leather boots. Leather boots regularly treated with skunk grease will remain soft and pliable and become near waterproof.

Horse liniment, too, has wonderful qualities. Use it to treat various external injuries of your horses and to solve various internal problems as well. Same for humans. A strained muscle, a sore back, rub on a little liniment. An upset stomach, a little liniment diluted in water will do wonders.

Be careful about too much bathing. A bath on Saturday night, before going to town, is sufficient. Too much water will weaken you, sap the strength right out of your muscles. Consider how you feel when you go swimming. Most people are worn out. The same thing can happen to you if you spend too much time in a bathtub.

Walk whenever and wherever you can. You'll see more, learn more, have an opportunity to think more, and besides you'll feel better.

Avoid constantly looking for an ache or a pain. If you keep looking you will likely find something, some kink, some difficulty on which to dwell, and cause you to worry and take your mind away from more constructive things.

- Learn to laugh again. Most of us have forgotten how. Try to laugh out loud at least once every day—several times if possible. There is nothing more fulfilling than a good laugh, the kind that starts down in your belly and grows.

- Laugh when your uncle tells you that on the first warm days in spring at the lumber camp, the lumberjacks took off their underwear and piled it by the river's edge. When the bedbugs went for a drink, the lumberjacks quickly grabbed up their bug-free underwear and ran back to the bunkhouse.

- Learn to laugh at yourself.

Food

- Eat plain food.

- Eat your largest meal at noon. Call it dinner, not lunch. Lunch is what you eat after playing cards in the evening at a relative's, or what the neighbor serves after you help butcher a pig. Supper is what you eat in the early evening, when the outdoor work for the day is finished, and before you do the evening milking.

- Eat food from the garden. In winter, eat canned food from the garden, stored potatoes from the cellar, sauerkraut from the crock, and meat from the smoked ham that hangs alongside the cellar steps. Enjoy fresh venison after the deer hunting season.

- Avoid "store-bought bread;" there is no power in it. Make bread from flour which is purchased by the fifty-pound sack. The empty sack can be used for making dresses, towels, and sometimes stuffed toys.

- In July, search for wild black raspberries in the woods. Tolerate the mosquitoes and scratches for the best berries are often in the deepest tangle of brush.

Watch out for black wasps, the kind that build a paper-like nest. They have the most wicked of bites and the fiercest of tempers. Avoid them.

Stay out of taverns.

Keep a few bottles of beer in your refrigerator. Nothing tastes better at the end of a long, hot day in summer than a cold beer. Be careful of the beer you buy. There is great difference among the brands. Buy a local beer. It generally has more flavor and gumption than the thinned out national brands.

Follow moderation in all things, except for family, care for the land, and concern for neighbors. In these matters be excessive.

Drink water fresh from a well. The less distance the water flows from its source to you, the better it tastes. The best water of all comes from the pump after it has been running for an hour or so, filling the cattle tank. All of the pipes are then as cold as the water; the sweetness of well water is enhanced by its coldness.

Never criticize the cook or the cooking.

Sleeping

Avoid spending too much time in bed, after all, most people die there.

Two hours of sleep before midnight are worth more than four hours after.

Early to bed and early to rise probably won't increase your wealth or your wisdom, but it will do wonders for your health.

Resist the temptation to dawdle in bed once you wake up. When you wake up, get up.

Unhappiness

To overcome unhappiness:

- Don't create problems when none exist.
- Worry about important things; the little things aren't worth the effort worrying requires.
- Don't make little problems into big problems.
- Smile more than frown.
- Enjoy the present rather than always looking for happiness in the future.
- Discount believing that the more things you accumulate, the happier you'll be.
- Avoid assuming that if only the government, your spouse, the weather—you fill in the blank—would change, you would be a happier person.

Putting Aside the "What Ifs"

Most of us spend far too much time fretting over what might have been, if only we had done something differently. For example, what if we had:

Planted more acres of corn because the crop we raised turned out so well.

Harvested the oat crop a day earlier and avoided the hail storm that destroyed most of it.

Remembered to close the barnyard gate so we didn't have to spend an hour rounding up the heifers.

Held our temper when Junior did something wrong.

We also project our "What ifs" into the future, allowing them to take up much of our thinking time, and disturbing our mental state.

- What if we don't get enough rain this summer?

- What if a cow gets sick?

- What if the price of milk goes down?

- What if the old tractor doesn't make it through the summer?

One way to handle the "what ifs" is to consider the worst possible thing that could happen if the "what if" comes true, and what we could do about it. Thinking this way, many of our "what if" fears disappear.

Complaining

- Facing a problem is easier than complaining about it.

- For some people finding the negative in life and complaining about it is easier than discovering the positive and applauding it.

- The world is what we make it. What is important is how we react to the world that we see, rather than doing nothing but complain.

- Take time to look at a daisy. Daisies grow on dry land and wet, alongside highways and in open fields. They come in blue and white, in yellow and pink. They are often chewed off, clipped off, stomped on and picked. Yet they always come back, in full color, with nary a complaint.

For The Bad Days

- Go fishing. Find a quiet lake where you can sit and watch your bobber, and think, or not think.

- Go ice fishing as often as you can. Sitting on a frozen lake in winter with a few old friends is a wonderful time to swap stories, and, in the quiet of a dark and dreary winter day, reflect on life.

Occasionally you will catch fish: a northern pike or a perhaps a perch or a bluegill. The taste of fish from a frozen lake is beyond description.

- Whittle. You don't have to make anything. A pile of wood shavings on the floor is an accomplishment, especially when everything seems to be going wrong.

- Scrub the kitchen floor, on your hands and knees, with a brush. Anger, frustration, whatever is bothering you will disappear—and you'll have a clean floor, too.

- Bake bread from scratch.

- Walk around your land. All the way around the boundaries. You could tell your spouse you're checking the fences. Maybe you are, but not the one's with fence posts.

8

Home-Grown Food

When I was growing up on a farm, the idea of buying vegetables from a grocery story never crossed my mother's mind. She tended a large garden that grew in a plot behind the house next to the woods that stretched to the north. The garden contained about every vegetable that would grow in our county: several rows of sweet corn, tomatoes, green beans, peas, carrots and cabbage—vegetables that could be canned and savored during the long winter months. Lesser vegetables like eggplant and peppers were there too, but in shorter rows. Of course pumpkins and squash had their place—they could be stored in our dirt floor cellar until Christmas and sometimes a little after. My father cultivated the garden a few times with a one horse cultivator, and later with the tractor. From my mother's perspective, he could never do it right. The heavy-footed horse and the tractor's tires did flatten some of my mother's favorite vegetables, and my father heard about it. But overall, the garden grew well. Here is some garden wisdom:

- Take a little time to plan your garden each year. It doesn't have to be fancy—a back of an envelope is fine, but do some planning.
- Plant your garden as early as possible. Depending on how far north you are, some of the early crops such as radishes, lettuce, peas, and early potatoes can go in the ground in late April or early May. Leave behind the notion that you must plant the entire garden at once. Best to plant it over several weeks, with the latest crops planted being the late sweet corn

and tomatoes that can't stand even a hint of late spring frost before they curl up, turn brown and die. If the ground is too cold, seeds such as squash and sweet corn won't germinate. So watch the spring temperatures and plant accordingly. In most years, much of the garden should be in by Memorial Day.

Garden planning principles to keep in mind:

- Don't plant tomatoes in the same place each year. Moving them around on your garden plot helps to control blight and other pesky tomato diseases.
- Keep the cucumbers away from the squash, gourds, and zucchini plants. These more aggressive vine plants will overrun the cucumbers. You won't be able to find the few cukes that do grow in the tangle of vines.
- Keep the sweet corn away from the popcorn; they'll cross-fertilize and you'll have both strange sweet corn and unusual popcorn.
- Plant the tomatoes so they are open to any breeze that flows across the garden. The summer breezes help to dry out the plants from the morning dews and summer showers, and keep down tomato blight. One way to do this is to plant peas and lettuce near the tomatoes. When the peas and lettuce are harvested, pull the plants, leaving more room for the tomatoes.
- Plant some marigolds in your garden, at least a row or two. They tend to keep insects away, and provide a nice floral display from late summer until frost.

- Plant raspberry plants so you can cultivate around them. This you will need to do regularly throughout the growing season, or one day you'll discover that your entire garden has become a raspberry bed.

- As you plant each row, push a stick into the ground at the end of it. Black locust sticks work well because they don't rot easily, and thus can be used year after year. Fasten the empty seed packet to the stick, then you'll remember what you planted.

- If you are a bit more organized, you may want to create a map of your garden as you plant it. Your plan was a guide. Your map is the real thing. This way you will know for sure what is planted where, even when the rain and wind tear away the empty seed packets.

- After you have harvested your early sweet corn, cut the corn plants into small pieces and leave them in the garden for mulch. Cutting down the plants allows sunlight to reach parts of your garden the corn plants may have shaded.

- Leave the tops of the beets, radishes, and carrots in the garden for mulch.

- In the late summer, when sections of the garden have been harvested, work up the soil and plant oats, wheat or rye. By the time the garden is ready for plowing in late October or early November, the grain crops will have grown a few inches tall and provide excellent green manure for your garden. Most gardens are severely lacking in organic matter which green manure provides.

Make sure you have some rhubarb—pieplant some people call it. It is the first to come in the spring, almost shooting out of the ground with the first warm sunny days. It makes great sauce, even better pie. Some say it is a blood purifier; eaten in the spring it cleanses the body from the accumulations of a long winter. It requires almost no tending, but comes back each spring with elephant-ear-size leaves and beautiful pink stalks.

Start a couple rows of asparagus, and be patient for the first couple years while it is becoming established. Then look forward each spring to a succulent feast as the slender stalks push out of the ground, and grow inches a day.

Include potatoes in your garden, at least three kinds. Early red ones for eating with fresh peas, late white ones for storing in the cellar, and russet potatoes for baking. Sow a few radish seeds at the beginning and end of each potato row. They will help you find the rows for cultivating because the radishes will come up long before the potatoes break the ground. Additionally, sow at least three short rows of radishes (long white ones, solid red ones, and those red on top and white on the bottom).

Plant carrots with some of the radishes. After the radishes are harvested, the carrots will flourish—and require little or no thinning.

Grow at least three kinds of sweet corn—very early, mid-season and late. That way you'll have fresh sweet corn for much of the summer.

Start tomatoes indoors on St. Patrick's Day, the day for celebrating green—and the Irish, too. Don't be fussy about the planting. Dump some clean soil in a garden pot; sprinkle on the tomato seeds. Cover them with enough soil so the seeds aren't poking out, then put the pots in a south-facing window, keep the soil moist, and in a week or so little tomato plants will peek out. Leave them in the garden pots until garden planting time. Don't worry much about thinning. The main thing is to keep them watered. When you set them out they'll look scraggly and mostly miserable. In a week or two they'll compete with the best store-bought tomato plants. In late summer, when the tomatoes hang red and heavy, pick them carefully to avoid bruises, and make tomato soup and tomato juice cocktail from them. Enjoy your tomatoes all year round in this way.

Plant several kinds of squash. Also include some pumpkins, peas, and green beans. Cauliflower is a little too fussy to fool with. Brussels sprouts and broccoli never had much appeal. Grow them if you must.

Don't over plant zucchini squash. Given half a chance, and a decent growing year, you'll have enough zucchini to feed everyone in your township. Try new ways to fix this sometimes maligned vegetable. It is a wonderful ingredient for baking, fries well, tastes good raw, too.

Plant some rutabagas. They grow best on breaking soil, that has been plowed for the first time. Plow a few furrows on the edge of the woods where the oaks were earlier cut. Scatter the rutabaga seed and stay out of the way. No hoeing, no fertilizing, no care of any kind. In fall, dig the 'bagas, as they are fondly called, with a six-tined fork and store them in the cellar. Nothing tastes better than a rutabaga or two in a kettle of vegetable soup, or cooked with some pork hocks, or even cooked by themselves and served like potatoes. Be sure you eat all the 'bagas before the first hot weather of spring. A spoiled rutabaga competes well with a rotten egg. A couple bushels of spoiled

50¢
Each
Spagetti
Squash
75

rutabagas will give your house an aroma that will live with you for months. Like an unwelcome guest who never bathes, except much worse.

Onions are a must, and cucumbers and dill for dill pickle making must also be included in your garden.

Plant some decorative popcorn. The type that has all red ears (strawberry corn) that can be placed in a wooden bowl along with a few small gourds for a nice fall display.

Don't forget a few hills of gourds. A couple or three hills is all you need as the vines grow the best of any vine crop in your garden. In a good year they'll climb right over the top of the pumpkins and even up and over the sweet corn, making a tangled mess. But all anger toward the competitive vine disappears when you find the many multi-colored and multi-shaped gourds in the fall.

Set out a strawberry patch. Eat strawberries three times a day in June, on your cornflakes for breakfast, in strawberry shortcake for dinner, as strawberries and cream or maybe a strawberry pie for supper. Make a strawberry sandwich for lunch anytime. To make a strawberry sandwich, pick five or six lush large red strawberries. Place them on a thick slice of buttered homemade bread, smash the strawberries with a dinner fork, sprinkle on a little sugar, cover with a second slice of bread. Eat hardy.

Grow some horseradish. Back of the chicken house is a good place to plant the roots. The chickens, in their everyday scratching, keep the weeds down but don't seem to bother the horseradish at all. Make horseradish sauce.

Learn to make wine—from strawberries, grapes, blackberries—that which you grow or can easily find on your land.

Grow flowers in your garden. Dahlias, gladiolas, and zinnias are particularly good choices. An old-fashioned rosebush is also nice, the kind that requires no care, comes back each year with a flurry of bright red flowers, and doesn't mind when the temperature dips below minus twenty in January.

Try a row of sunflowers along the edge of your garden. They grow fast and soon yellow faces will greet you each day, besides providing much desired bird food.

Don't forget cabbage. You'll need lots of it if you want to make sauerkraut—fifteen heads at least. Nothing tastes better on a cool day in autumn than homemade sauerkraut. Here's how to make it.

Homemade Sauerkraut

What is needed:

- Large-headed white cabbage, 6 pounds or more per head.
- Non-iodized salt. Coarse pickling salt works well. The purpose of the salt is to draw the juice out of the cabbage so it will ferment.
- A large sharp knife to shred the cabbage if a kraut cutter is not available.
- An earthenware crock from 2 1/2 to 20 gallons, depending on how much sauerkraut you wish to make.
- A covering consisting of several layers of coarse cheese cloth or muslin which is placed between the cut cabbage and a china plate that is large enough to cover the cabbage and fit within the crock.
- A rock or clean brick to weigh down the plate. The covering and the weight are used to bring the brine to the surface of the shredded kraut. It is important to keep oxygen out of the crock as it will cause spoilage. Keep all metal away from the process.

Procedure:

- Remove the coarse outer leaves from the cabbage. Do not wash the heads because the natural bacteria found there are necessary for the fermentation process.
- Cut the heads into halves and then quarters. Slice to obtain as long a shred as possible.
- Place the shredded cabbage in layers in the crock. For every layer of three to four pounds of cabbage sprinkle 2 1/2 tablespoons of salt.
- After every two or three layers, pound the shredded cabbage with a stick of wood until juice appears.
- Fill the container within four or five inches of the top. Position the cloth covering over the kraut and lap it over the edge of the container. Place the snug-fitting china plate on the cloth.
- Finally, put the weight on the plate. The action of the salt will draw the juice out of the cabbage and make a brine which will rise to the top. Mold may appear on the top of the brine. Remove it daily.
- In three to five days remove the cover and check the progress. Some discoloration due to spoilage may appear on the top inch or so. Remove it. Also, rinse the cloth before replacing it.
- Store the fermenting kraut in a well-ventilated place with a temperature of from 68 to 72 degrees F. At this temperature the kraut should be ready for eating in six to eight weeks. If stored in a cool place it may take several months. The kraut will not ferment when the temperature is below freezing, but will start fermenting again when the temperature warms.
- The fermented kraut will keep indefinitely in the crock as long as the top is not exposed to the open air.
- The kraut may be removed from the crock, placed in freezer bags and stored in the refrigerator for several months. It may also be frozen or canned.

Broomcorn Brooms

Plant a short row of broomcorn. Broomcorn grows with its seeds on the top of the bristles that you can later make into fireplace brooms, or full-size brooms if you want. The seeds make excellent bird feed.

It's not difficult to make your own brooms out of broomcorn you grow in your garden. Here are directions for doing it:

1. Start with the heads from ten or a dozen broomcorn plants. Comb out the seeds that are on the ends of the bristles. Save the seeds for the birds, and some for planting next year.

2. Fasten the heads together at the top, leaving the bristles on the bottom. Hay wire, or any other wire that won't break when you twist it, will work fine. Three or four pieces of wire should be enough. Slip a piece of leather throng under the top wire before you tighten it. The leather throng will provide a way to hang up your broom. A leather shoelace makes a perfect leather throng for your broom. With a sharp knife, square off the ends of the bristles so they are all the same length. What you have made is a whisk broom for cleaning in the corners, and brushing off the furniture.

3. *A variation.* Follow steps one and two, until you get to the place where you are tightening the wire around the broomcorn heads. This time fasten the broomcorn heads around a handle made from a ¾-inch stick, 18 inches long. Black locust works particularly well, but almost any wood will suffice—willow and ash would also be choices. With a jackknife, cut a few grooves in the part of the stick where you are fastening the broomcorn heads. This will help prevent the broomcorn from slipping off the stick when everything dries out and shrinks a little. Now you have what some people call a fireplace broom. A longer handle, and a few more broomcorn heads, and you'll have a regular, full-size broom. Try different lengths of handles, and different amounts of broomcorn. Great fun for a rainy day in fall, with the rain splashing on the shed roof.

9

Taking Life As It Comes

Rural people have long known that too much of anything, whether it is work, rainfall, or a city relative's visit, is not good and leads to problems. Also, because so much of what happens in the country is caused by something beyond a person's control—weather, markets, sick animals—flexibility is needed. To take life as it comes:

- Enjoy being alone; enjoy being with others.
- Keep up with what is happening in the world. Read more than one newspaper; it's always good to have a second opinion, particularly when it comes to farming, politics and religion.
- Avoid crowds, loud talking, big cities, and boastful people.
- Don't be too taken by churches and preachers. God is in many places; the church is just one of them. Being religious on Monday through Saturday is more important than being religious on Sunday. It's easy on Sunday, not so easy the rest of the week.
- Be optimistic. Even when the bottom leaves of the corn are drying, and the haymows are only half full there is always next year with its promise and mystery, its hope and anticipation, and if not next year, the year after that.
- Do the best you can with what you've got.
- Doing things "straight" leads to clear thinking, and points you in an uncluttered

direction. Doing things straight means building a straight fence, shocking grain in straight rows, plowing a straight furrow, and planting corn rows that run north and south or east and west, never on the diagonal.

- Sometimes circling is the better way to go. For instance, when trying to convince a neighbor of something, it is usually better to circle around the topic a couple of times than to blurt out what you have on your mind. A good place to start is with the weather, then move to talking about crops, and cows, and the terrible state of the world, then ease into the topic you really wanted to talk about. Your neighbor will know what you are doing. You'll both enjoy the process, even though it takes lots of time, and often doesn't lead to any mind changing. Sometimes it does.

- Success is not forever.

- Better to downplay success than gloat about it. Even when you are having a good year—the rains have come regularly, the first cutting of hay was tall and lush, and the corn crop looks promising—it is better to reply, when asked how things are going, "Could be worse," rather than saying something like "Outstanding," or "Couldn't be better." You just never know when a hailstorm will ruin the corn crop or lightning will strike the barn and burn it to the ground.

- Answer an ad for a "surprise offer." But don't be disappointed with the item when it arrives—be surprised.

- Dream big dreams. But be careful. Consider the consequences of your dreams coming true.

- Know your history—where you were born, where you grew up—but don't dwell on it. Only you can decide what view to take on your past, what to share, what to forget.

- Living in the past can be as harmful to your mental state as living in the future. Both are important places to visit, but don't forget the present.

- Look for humor in everything that you do and everything that goes on around you.

- A hobby gives your mind a rest from your work—fishing, hiking, reading, sewing, weaving, carving, or fixing an old engine. What it is doesn't matter. What's important is taking an interest in something beyond your work.

- Go for a swim in a nearby lake on a hot evening in July, after the milking is done and there is a still a couple hours of daylight. Take the whole family.

- Remember to listen for the whispers and look in the shadows.

- It is often better to see things as they are than to try and change them.

- Avoid looking at things as other people say you should see them. You are entitled to your own view.

- Go to a polka dance. Dance the schottische, an old-time waltz, a circle two-step, and the flying Dutchman. Dance every polka. Your troubles will lift with each beat, and you'll return home exhausted, but refreshed.

- Appreciate how the leader of the polka band can play the fiddle with a finger missing from his left hand.

- Tackle a small problem when you first notice it. A small problem ignored can become a large problem not easily solved. The tendency is to overlook the little problems until they become big, and then panic and declare a crisis.

- It takes time for the mud to settle in a murky stream, just as it takes time for the mud to settle in our daily lives.

Time

- Time is the changing of the seasons, the first flock of geese in the spring, the call of the whippoorwill on a hot summer evening, the sound of crickets in early fall, the silence of winter. Time in the country is not clocks and watches.

- Time is sunset and sunrise, when the corn is planted and the tomatoes are ready for canning, when the moon is full and when there is no moon at all.

- Time is when the children are ready to leave home, when your hair turns gray and it takes twice as long to do something than when you were younger.

- Time is experience and wisdom, yesterday and tomorrow. Time is also right now, this moment.

- Time is not the same as money, as some would suggest.

- Be on time, a little early if possible, no matter if you are going to church or to an ice cream social. Set all your clocks and watches ahead fifteen minutes. Then you will have a time cushion, but you will never know exactly what time it is, for clocks tend to gain and lose. Setting your clocks ahead will assure that you and your spouse will always have something to discuss—"What time do you think it really is?"

- We all have the same number of hours in each day. Why do some of us run out of time sooner than others?

Little Things

- Appreciate a warm floor to put your feet on when the temperature outside is below zero.

- Enjoy a fountain pen for writing. There is something about the flow of ink on paper that adds to the experience of writing, beyond the message you are trying to convey.

- Buy shoes that fit, even if you must pay a few extra dollars. There is nothing that contributes more to a sour disposition than sore feet.

- Being comfortable is more important than being stylish.

- Read a good book, slowly, allowing the words to roam around in your mind and stir up your thinking and your feelings.

- Talk with a three-year-old, especially if he is your grandson. Listen carefully to the words, and the perspectives and wisdom he conveys. Three-year-olds move to the core of matters, in their thinking and in their communication.

- Own a comfortable chair. You only need one, and when you find it, keep it. If your spouse tells you it has become shabby and unsightly, resist the temptation to buy a new one. It often takes years to break in a chair. If an unsightly chair becomes a problem for appearances, such as when the preacher is planning a visit, toss a bed-spread over it. When the preacher leaves, yank off the cover, sink back into your chair and be comfortable. Hard to be comfortable when the preacher is visiting anyway.

- Freshly ground pepper is a treat for every meal. Nothing improves the taste of good food more. Avoid salt. Most food already has too much.

Take Time

- Take time to do nothing. To sit quietly. To clear your mind. Set aside the clutter of the day's activity, and allow your mind to go blank. Do this several times a day.

- Take time to dream. Dream about what might be, what will never be, and what shouldn't be. Too much doing with too little dreaming leads to boredom.

- Take time to discover your family roots—where your parents were born and what

their growing up years were like. Learn about your grandparents and their parents. What were their stories? To know who we are and where we are headed, we must know where we've been—we must know our family roots.

- Take time to paint a picture, sit under an oak tree, watch the sun set, smell an apple blossom, play with your grandchild.

- Take time to listen for the sound of a church bell announcing the beginning of services, for the roar of a snowplow grinding along your drifted road.

- Take time to listen to the snapping and cracking of a stick of pine wood in your stove, to the lonesome whistle of a locomotive as it approaches country road crossings.

- Take time to listen for a hoot owl far off in the woods to the north, the call of a sandhill crane in the marsh by the river, the low rumble of thunder on a hot, humid night in July.

- Take time to listen for the quiet "dong," "dong," of the bell on the neighbor's cow in night pasture, the chirping of hundreds of crickets on a warm night in early September, the laughter of children playing in the schoolyard just down the road.

- Take time to hear the robin song in early spring, waves lapping on the shore of the lake, the creaking of an empty barn, a word of praise from your mother-in-law, the cooing of a two-month old baby.

- Take time to hear your daughter practicing scales on the old piano that has been in your family for three generations, and the gentle lowing of a cow for her newborn calf.

Do Something Different

- Doing something different from the routine of everyday life gives us a new perspective, wakes us up, shows us the familiar

in new ways, and helps us appreciate what we have.

- Visit a big city. Look to the top of the tall buildings and not care what others may think about your gazing. Watch the city at night, the thousands of bright lights everywhere, and wonder what the view must have been before electricity. Listen to the sounds of the city, the sirens and impatient car horns, the roar of truck engines and the clatter of commuter trains. Walk on a busy street among the hundreds of people hurrying this way and that, most with serious, determined looks on their faces.

- Walk on an Atlantic Ocean beach. Look for seashells. Listen to the surf that never stops, even when there is no wind. Look to the horizon and wonder what your ancestors must have felt when they landed in this country, and realized that when they arrived on these shores they knew that they would likely never return to their place of birth.

- Stand on the shores of Lake Superior in a November storm, when the wind sends mountainous waves crashing on the shore, causing the ore boat captains to have second thoughts about their chosen careers.

- Climb a mountain. It doesn't have to be a tall one, just tall enough so you can see over the tops of the trees, and the roads, and the fields that spread out below you.

- Go barefoot for an hour. Walk in the grass and allow it to sneak up between your toes. Feel the coolness on a hot day in summer.

- Take a canoe ride on a quiet lake. Rest the paddle and drift.

- Listen to classical music, or country tunes, or rock—whatever you've decided you don't like.

- Visit the far North. Spend a night in Beaver Creek, Yukon Territory and become acquainted with the Alaskan Highway.

- Volunteer some time at your local library.

- Spend a day a month helping out at your local historical society.

- Travel to another country. Avoid comparing what you see with what you have at home. See what you see for what it is, not how it is better or worse than something with which you are familiar.

- Plant some Mexican corn that grows twenty feet tall, and a few hills of squash that can weigh upwards of two hundred pounds. When your brother-in-law asks, "Why?" answer, "Why not?"

- Spend an evening with a neighbor's aging parent, so they can have some time to themselves.

- Write a few lines of poetry. It doesn't matter if the words rhyme or not. What matters is that you express your feelings which is the real stuff of poetry.

- Learn some words in another language. The more you know another language, the better you'll understand your own.

- Start a journal. In it record the weather. Write down the activities of the day, the good and the bad, the joys and disappointments, and your feelings toward it all. As you write, a great load will often lift from your shoulders. You'll have a record that you can go back to, to see what your life was like at an earlier age.

10

Getting Along and Politicians

Living in the country means getting along with all kinds of folks. You never know when you might need someone to help you out. Neighbors are especially prized. When I was growing up we had neighbors representing several ethnic groups—Germans, Norwegians, Welsh, Bohemians, Polish, English, and an array of religious persuasions. Some were Lutheran, several Catholic, a handful of Methodists and Baptists, and a few who belonged to no church and were quite proud of it. Some were good farmers, several so-so, and a couple families ought to have been doing something else, but they continued to struggle along, never quite learning how farming worked.

One family had become thieves, stealing wrenches from machinery left in the field, and committing other dishonest acts. We all knew who they were, and we simply avoided leaving our wrenches in our machines. No one ever considered reporting them to the sheriff. After all, they were our neighbors.

Of course there are many other people to get along with beyond the neighbors. It was important to be on good terms with the business people in town: the miller who ground our cow feed, the grocer who traded our eggs for groceries, the blacksmith who pounded out our plow points and fixed our always-breaking machinery, and a host of others. We depended on them—they depended on us, too, of course.

Not everyone got along. People got into arguments with each other, and sometimes wouldn't talk for years; this included neighbors and former friends, and especially relatives. Sometimes it was hard for the kids when they heard from their parents, "Oh, you can't go fishing with Johnny, we don't have anything to do with those people." You'd gotten to know Johnny in school and he seemed like a good guy.

Neighbors

- Good fences make for good neighbors.
- Try to do more for your neighbors than they do for you.
- When your neighbors need help, drop whatever you are doing and help them.
- A handshake is as good as a written contract; easier, too, and you don't have to fish around through a cluttered bureau drawer trying to find the piece of paper to write the words. Be clear about on what you agree. If you have questions ask them before you shake hands.
- A promise made is a promise kept. To "go back on your promise" is next to lying.
- Consider everyone honest until they show you otherwise.
- Treat everyone the same, no matter what color their skin, their politics, their religion or lack of it.
- To shout back when you are shouted at allows the other person to take control of the interchange.
- Nothing quells a disagreement faster than refusing to raise your voice to those who raise their voice to you.
- Overlook bad manners, disagreeable behavior, and lack of responsiveness the first time. Everyone has a bad day.
- The best thing to do in many situations is to do nothing.
- It is often best to say nothing and be thought stupid than to open your mouth and remove all doubt.
- If you can't say something good about someone, say nothing at all.

Decker
Tours
Nagel Lumber's
LOG PULL CLASSIC

Being Yourself

- Be yourself, don't pretend to be who you are not.
- Always striving for the approval of others is to have your compass set in the wrong direction.
- In our haste to seek approval from others, we overlook searching for approval of ourselves.
- We gain respect by earning it.
- Few things are more important than your name. One blemish on your name does more to discredit you than a lifetime of achievement will help people think well of you.
- It is the outside of a person that we see, but what's inside is most important.
- As hard as we may try, no one ever fools a child.

Strangers and Friends

- When strangers appear at your door, invite them in and offer them a cup of coffee. Another day you may be a stranger knocking on an unknown door.
- When fixing a meal, always be prepared to set one more place, and sometimes more than one, at the table. You can never tell who will drop by, and to not offer them food if they arrive at mealtime would be rude.
- If you arrive at someone's house at mealtime, the polite thing to do is to accept a cup of coffee and perhaps dessert, but not eat the entire meal.
- Accept all people as good, unless they say something or do something that changes your opinion.
- Urban strangers and salespeople are those who trek up to your never-used front door and search for a doorbell that is

not there. Some realize, after the first embarrassing moments, that they are trying to enter where no one has entered before, and find their way around to the kitchen door. Treat them as the strangers they are. Avoid judging them, for they know not the ways of country people.

- Be wary of the salesperson who takes too much for granted, such as the vacuum cleaner salesman who insists on spreading his little bag of dirt on the living room floor to demonstrate the prowess of his machine, only to discover a moment later that the farmer does not have electricity.

- Friends are always there, even when you don't need them.

- Visit a friend in a nursing home. You will bring joy to their lives, and you'll gain a new appreciation for yours.

Politicians

Rural politicians have long been the brunt of jokes, yet they are also prized for helping rural people live with the rules and regulations that abound in the countryside, as they do everywhere else.

- Many politicians talk and talk, with the hope that they will think of something to say.

- Don't expect a politician to do after he is elected, what he said he would do while running for office.

- As the wind blows, so the politician bends.

- Many politician's backbones are as stiff as an ice cube in boiling water. In the beginning it is there, but it soon disappears, in a puff of steam.

- When we blame politicians, we should blame ourselves, especially if we failed to vote when they were elected.

- A politician with a tax dollar is like a child in a candy store.

- One-room country school boards were politicians at their best. They knew what they were supposed to do. They knew why, and they knew who they reported to—their neighbors. They also knew that the decisions they made affected the future of the country, for what is more important than the education of our children?

11

Conundrums and Other Wise Bits

When something sounded a little strange and difficult to figure out, my mother would say, "It's a conundrum." Today, some people would call these paradoxes. Conundrum has a better sound to it.

- Let's all stick together, everybody for himself.
- Our strength can be our weakness, our weakness is often our strength.
- Doing less can mean doing more.
- Not knowing can be the highest level of knowing.
- The longest road somewhere can be the shortest.
- That which is most hidden from us is often most present.
- Sometimes the harder we think about something, the less we understand it.
- Staying behind sometimes is the best route for getting ahead.
- The greatest light can come from darkness.
- To become full you may need to first become empty.
- The brighter you shine your light, the dimmer becomes your lantern.
- Taking charge often means letting go.

- Sometimes the harder you look the less you see.

- To know what you believe, you must know what you don't believe.

- When you come to a fork in the road, take it.

- The smoother the road, the firmer we should grip the steering wheel.

Your Surroundings

- Paint your house, barn and outbuildings regularly. Keep everything around your buildings neat and tidy. Your farmstead is a window on who you are and what you value.

- Plant a few trees every year, even if you know they may never provide you shade or firewood. There are always children and grandchildren to enjoy them, if not yours, someone else's.

- Consider carefully before cutting a tree someone says is in the way. It takes a hundred years to grow a tree and fifteen minutes to saw it down.

Traveling Country Roads

- For many trips the first step is the most difficult, but no matter how long the trip, it always begins with that first step.

- Some trips are two steps forward and one back, better this arrangement than the opposite.

- The size of the cloud of dust tells us little about the traveler.

- It is better to be making dust than traveling in the dust someone else has made.

- We are often so intent on our destination that we overlook the beauty along the way.

WARNING

- There is probably a reason a road is less traveled. However, the less traveled road may be the one to take.

- An unpaved road is a thing of beauty, until the dust sifts into your house every time a car passes.

- Some roads are made for traveling slowly, for contemplation along the way, for thinking deep thoughts. These roads slow you down and help you realize that by moving less quickly there is another side to life, and to living.

- You can't know where you are going until you know where you are.

- Some of the most difficult trips we make occur without ever leaving home.

- Crossing a border in our mind is often more difficult than crossing a border into another country.

- When we travel we often learn more about where we live than we learn about the place we visit.

- The road home is often the longest.

- It is usually a rough and crooked road to the top of the hill.

When traveling country roads look for:

- The spires of country churches, often the highest points in the countryside. In the minds of many, they point the way to God.

- Closed country schools, some of them now homes, that dotted the Midwest by the thousands until they were closed in the name of educational reform and "better advantages" for country children.

- Abandoned cheese factories, located where cattle were raised and milk produced. They were close enough together so a farmer could haul his milk to the cheese factory with his team, and still get home in time to do a day's work on the farm.

Clumps of lilac bushes, standing alone alongside the road. Generally they were part of a farmstead, now bulldozed over as farms grew larger and farm buildings got in the way of "progress." But the lilacs remained, silent reminders of an earlier day when the farm family looked forward to the sweet smelling purple flowers each spring.

12

Seasonal Changes

Seasonal change dramatically influences the lives of those who live in the north. Upper midwesterners enjoy each season, mostly, but there is always complaining and an anticipation of the coming season. This is especially so with winter, the longest of the four. A hot summer, not uncommon, also evokes complaints and fond memories of colder weather, the same kind of weather that was criticized only a few months earlier.

Spring

In spring we shake loose the shackles of winter and make big plans and think big thoughts. We celebrate what has passed and look forward to the future with joy and hope. In no other season is there such anticipation. Spring is melting snow and mud. Mud in the road. Mud in the fields. Mud tracked into the kitchen. Spring is maple syrup and flooding streams, green grass and frisky calves, open windows and cows on pasture.

- In spring listen for melt water dripping from a snowy roof.
- Listen for Canada geese winging north.
- Listen for pond frogs making a noisy production of spring's arrival.
- Listen for a ruffed grouse drumming on a log deep in the woods.
- Listen for the first robin's song.

- Listen for the creaking of harness leather as the team of horses pulls a walking plow.
- Smell freshly turned soil after the plow has tipped a furrow.
- Smell bed sheets that have hung on the clothesline for a couple hours.
- Smell the blossoms of wild cherry, plum, apple and black locust.
- Feel the sunshine on your back when you hike to the still frozen pond.
- Feel a March wind that tears the dead oak leaves off the trees and sends dry leaves scurrying across the yard.
- Feel the first spring rain on your face.
- Watch cows kick up their heels when they are turned out to pasture for the first time after months confined in the barn.
- Watch newly born kittens tumble over each other in their play.
- Look for the first oak leaves; they are a quiet green that soon takes over the color of the woodlot.

Summer

Summer is enduring heat and hungry insects, days beginning before dawn and ending after dark, never-ending work. Summer is bluegill fishing, swimming in the pond, and watching free outdoor movies in town on Tuesday night. Summer is often dry weather, when the sun shines day after day and the land becomes parched, when old-timers claim that during the driest years rivers run only on Tuesdays and Thursdays.

- In summer listen for wind blowing across a tall grass field.
- Listen for the rustle of corn leaves on a quiet night in August.

- Listen for the clattering of a hay mower slicing off alfalfa.

- A steel wheel hay wagon lumbering along a country road.

- The "pop" "pop," of the neighbor's John Deere B tractor.

- Listen for the gentle call of the holstein cow summoning her newborn calf.

- Listen for bullfrogs singing slow and deep, a strange but beautifully haunting tune.

- Listen for water gurgling along a rocky stream, moving from its meager beginnings upstream to eventually tumbling into the Atlantic Ocean.

- In summer smell fresh cut hay curing in the field.

- Fresh peas cooking on a wood stove.

- Horse sweat.

- Smell country road dust that hangs in the air when a car passes.

Fall

Fall means filling silo, husking corn and gathering orange pumpkins before the first hard freeze. Fall is squirrel hunting, apple picking and sorghum making. It is a gathering time as the crops are harvested, the cattle are herded into the barn, and the family collects around the kitchen stove to eat popcorn.

- In fall listen for the sound of the school bell echoing in the valley, announcing the beginning of the fall term.

- Listen for the barking of a gray squirrel on a quiet evening, just as the sun is setting.

- Listen for the hooting of an owl deep in the woods to the west, when there is no other sound.

- Hear a wild turkey gobbling, trying to impress the hens.

- Listen for the rustling of corn leaves in the shocks that march across the stubbled corn fields like so many tepees.

- Hear the corn shredder shudder as cob-heavy corn stalks are pushed into it, and yellow corn cobs tumble into the corn wagon, and crushed stalks and leaves fly out the blower pipe.

- In fall feel the first cold rain of the season splattering on your face as you go for the cows on a dreary October morning.

- Feel the frost underfoot when you walk to the barn for the early morning chores.

- Feel the smooth skin of a ripe apple before biting into it.

- Smell fallen leaves on the forest floor as you search for dead oak trees to cut for the wood stoves.

- Smell sorghum juice boiling in a kettle, the steam rising into the crisp fall air.

- Smell fresh sorghum smeared thick on Mother's homemade bread.

- Smell homemade vegetable soup simmering on the back of the wood burning cookstove, the aroma of soup mixing with a hint of wood smoke.

- Smell hay in the barn loft, the aroma of dried alfalfa, clover and timothy engulfing you as you fork hay from the mow to the eagerly awaiting cattle below.

- Smell newly dug potatoes piled high in the cellar under the house, a subtle earthy smell.

Winter

Winter is time for reflection, to take stock of the year that is past and the year that is coming. Winter is for relaxing, for reading a good book, for putting together a puzzle, for visiting with a friend, for taking a long walk. For slipping on a pair of skis and sliding across an open field. For pulling on a pair of skates and making a few rounds on the frozen pond, just to prove you can still do it.

- In winter listen for ice cracking on the pond, leaving fissures that spread across the expanse of the wind-swept surface. Mysterious sounds of protest.
- Listen to the howl of a blizzard which rattles the windows and piles snow high against the barn door.
- The creak and squeak of snow as you walk along the road on a below zero morning.
- The call of a lone crow on a quiet morning when there are no other sounds.
- The crunch of snow under snowshoes when you shuffle across a snow buried field.
- The laughter of children as they belly flop on their sleds and race down the long hill back of the schoolhouse.
- Listen to the crackling of wood burning in the wood stove, and the gentle sound of the steam rising from the teakettle.
- Feel the warmth of your favorite cap, and the comfort of your leather mittens with their home-knitted wool liners that have served you well for many winters.
- Look for the big dipper hanging in the northern sky on a snowy, clear, crisp night in winter. Wonder about the millions of stars that surround it, and where they came from, and, at the same time, wonder about where you came from.
- Learn to find the North Star, pointed to by the upper right star in the cup of the big dipper, and high in the northern sky. If you can find the North Star, even if you are lost, you at least know the directions.

 Be amazed by the northern lights when they appear across the northern horizon, as they often do in fall and winter. Beginning as a glow in the northern sky, they often become an extravaganza of shifting shafts of light and multiple colors, constantly changing, and always amazing.

 Stand in a snowstorm and allow the snow to pellet your face. Feel the power of the wind and the challenge of the cold. Recall the days when you walked a mile to school in a snowstorm, and all you could think of was the warmth of the schoolroom.

13

One With Nature

Living in the country means living close to nature. Seeing wild animals is an everyday occurrence, whether it is a white-tail deer standing in the field just outside the kitchen window, or a turkey gobbler strutting along the trail leading up the hill beyond the barn. Occasionally, nature comes a little too close for even a country person. One of those times is when a skunk builds a den under the back porch. Another is when a furry brown bat takes up residence in your attic, and on a warm summer evening wakes you up when it swoops around your bedroom, somehow lost on its way to the outside.

Nature comes too close when one of those beautiful deer sneaks into your vegetable garden and destroys an entire row of peas, plus most of the green beans, in one night. And then, a couple weeks later, a raccoon, appropriately wearing its black mask, emerges from the woods, steals into your garden, and ruins fifteen ears of new sweet corn.

But these are the exceptions, the low points in nature-human interactions. Most of the time the relationships are congenial, wild animals and humans living together, not excessively disrupting each other's lives.

Of course nature is more than deer, skunks, bats, and raccoons. And there is much more to a relationship with nature than encounters with wild animals.

Nature

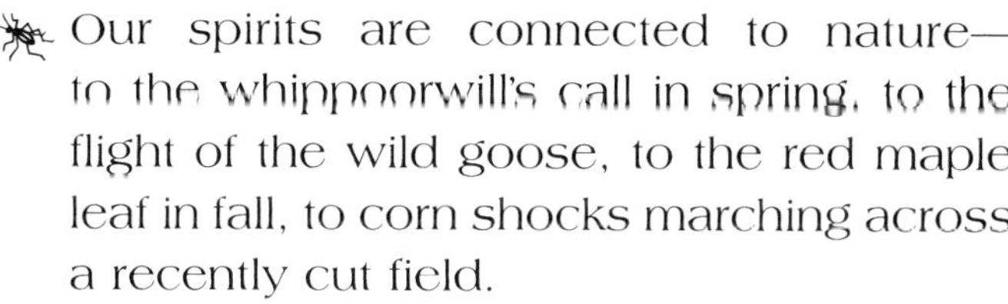

Our spirits are connected to nature—
to the whippoorwill's call in spring, to the
flight of the wild goose, to the red maple
leaf in fall, to corn shocks marching across
a recently cut field.

- Love the earth, but respect it, too. It will constantly delight and surprise.

- Care for your soul by allowing your inner self to become exposed, as the soul of the earth is exposed each time a furrow is turned. When the earth is plowed, new life appears. When you allow your inner self the light of day, personal growth occurs.

- Spend lots of time outdoors. Dig in a garden, sit under a tree, fish in a pond, split wood, watch a doe deer.

- Watch the sun set each night. It tells you about tomorrow's weather, but it also helps you celebrate the day's end with the promise of the sunrise.

- Take a grandchild for a walk in the woods. You'll both see more than either expected.

- Walk quietly in the outdoors; if you are with someone, don't talk. You will see and hear so much more.

- When you hear the flocks of migrating Canada geese each spring and fall, look upward. See the grace and beauty, cooperation and respect.

- Learn to tell the difference between oak, pine, cherry, hickory, locust, cedar, birch, and aspen wood by smell and touch.

- Master wood splitting. Discover how to read a block of wood, the direction of the grain, and the placement of the knots. Savor the sweet smell of fresh split oak, and relish the honest exercise that comes from swinging a splitting maul.

- Learn which firewood starts quickly (pine and cedar), and which wood heats hottest and longest (oak, hickory, and black locust).

- Walk in the woods when it's ten below zero. Listen to the quiet of the frozen forest, and then be surprised by the occasional rifle-loud cracks of wood fiber exploding from the cold.

- Listen for the death-like rattle of the dried oak leaves that hang on the trees in winter, as a cold wind sweeps across the snow-covered woods.

- Develop a healthy respect for wasps, hornets, and bumble bees.

- Learn to value snakes. They have an important place.

- Develop respect for bats. They do not fly into your hair, but catch mosquitoes—thousands of them. Applaud the furry little creatures, marvel at them, keep them working for you.

- Learn how to make a box trap. Trap a garden-raiding rabbit; haul it back into the woods and release it. If it's fall, enjoy some rabbit stew.

Beauty

- When you come upon a wild rose, or a wild plum tree in bloom, or even a red clover plant, stop and marvel at the colors and how they change as the sun plays on the flowers. Don't forget to put your nose to the blossoms and smell the subtle fragrances. Here is beauty at its finest.

- Walk to a high point on your farm, or in your neighborhood, or wherever you can find a lofty place. Look out over the landscape, at the trees, and the planted fields, at the farmsteads, the sky, the birds, and the clouds.

- Go to this same high place on a clear night, and look at the stars and the shadows, the blacks and grays, and the immensity of the universe. Consider how insignificant each of us is, on this earth and beyond.

The Wind

- Enjoy the wind. Feel it. Embrace it. But always respect it.

- Use wind direction to predict fishing success:
  - Wind from the west, fish bite the best.
  - Wind from the east, fish bite the least.
  - Wind from the south blows the hook right into the fish's mouth.
- Listen to the wind sift through the bare tree limbs of winter, making a lonely, sorrowful sound.
- Hear the summer wind softly caress the white pine needles, set the aspen leaves into nervous chatter, and cause the maple leaves to flutter like so many little fans.
- Listen to the creaks and squeaks of an old farm windmill on a windy night in fall, and allow your mind to create fearsome unknown creatures that are battling for the rights to the night.
- Watch the wind play with the surface of a pond, creating ripples and riffles that form and disappear.

Weather

Rural people have long been interested in the weather. What they do each day and the day after is affected by rain or sunshine, cold weather or warm, roaring winds or gentle breezes. It's the weather, largely, that determines a good year, an average year or a terrible year for a farmer. Is it any wonder that rural folks are always trying to figure out the weather that is coming? Here are some weather predictors that have been passed down from generation to generation.

- Rain before seven, stop before eleven.
- Red sky at night, no rain in sight.
- Red sky in morning, time to take warning.
- If the dog is eating grass, rain within twenty-four hours.
- No dew in the morning, rain before night.

- April showers bring May flowers.
- Rain in May is a barn full of hay.
- Rain in June is a silver spoon.
- The heavier a dog's hair in fall, the colder the winter.
- Little rainbows on each side of the sun (sun dogs) predict precipitation within forty-eight hours.
- A ring around the moon means a major change in the weather.
- A sliver of a new moon, tipped so you can't hang a pail of water on it means rain within twenty-four hours.
- If among the clouds, there is a patch of blue sky large enough to make a Dutchman's britches, clear weather is on the way.

Rain

- Delight in a rainy day. It is nature's way of cleansing and refreshing the land, and a time to relax from work that is now postponed.
- Enjoy a thunderstorm. Be awed at the power of lightning, and always be thankful for the rainfall. Some soil seems never to have enough rain.
- Climb the ladder to the haymow on a rare rainy day in July. Rest on the fresh hay, and listen to the raindrops drum on the roof overhead. Smell the aroma of sweet clover and alfalfa and feel the softness of the hay beneath you. Be thankful that you are alive, at this time, and in this place.

Milkweeds

- Pull a leaf from a milkweed plant in summer and catch the milky ooze on your finger. What other plant has such interesting life juice?

- Notice how monarch butterflies are attracted to the milkweed flowers; sometimes dozens of them congregate where milkweeds grow in profusion.

- Pick a milkweed pod in fall. Open it allowing the hundreds of seeds, each attached to its own little parachute, to float free.

- Recall when you were in school, painting empty milkweeds pods with gold or silver paint and giving them to your mother as Christmas tree ornaments.

Valley Pond

- Sit quietly by a pond, when the summer sun is sinking behind the trees and the birds are sharing their last quiet songs before day's end.

- Look for a doe and her fawn emerging out of the evening mists to drink at the pond's edge.

- Watch for a mother raccoon teaching her little masked furry offspring how to fish from shore.

- Listen for the slap of a beaver's tail breaking the silence of the evening, letting you know that beavers are aware of your presence.

- Feel the early evening breeze sifting across the clearing and washing over the pond, riffling the surface.

- See little fingers of fog lifting from the water and hanging motionless, like translucent curtains hanging in front of nature's stage.

- Watch a mallard duck ease away from shore toward mid-pond, followed by six little ducks, one behind the other, the exact same distance apart. Swimming lessons.

- Sit on the shore of the pond on a warm afternoon in October. Watch the reflections in the water as the sun plays on the red maples, yellow aspens, and browning oak leaves.

- Drop a pebble into a pond. Watch the splash and then the circles that form, ever larger, until they disappear—leaving the surface as smooth as before. When you're feeling overly important, think about the pebble, the splash and the circles.

14

Remembering

Remembering earlier days is more than nostalgia. Remembering helps people recall their roots, and their values. Many rural people live on land that was settled by ancestors three or four generations ago. A grandfather may have built their barn at the turn of the century. A great-grandfather probably cleared the twenty-acre field to the north, when he first arrived from Germany.

Memories of the past are all around, reminders that others have gone this way before—plowed the fields, harvested the grain, milked the cows, attended church, sent children to the one-room school, celebrated holidays, and did many things that rural people do today.

Sometimes it is fun to take time out, sit quietly and reflect on our memories. I'm sure some of my memories will evoke memories for you.

I remember, as a child, how important and special was a new pair of shoes, and how wonderful, too, was a new pair of bib overalls with their blue denim smell and freshness. How I resisted their washing, for in the washing some of their specialness was lost.

I remember my first day of school, when I was the smallest, youngest kid in the one-room country school (or so it seemed), and I sat quietly at my desk, the smell of freshly oiled floors engulfing me, and the idea of spending eight years here overwhelming me.

I remember the country mill that was powered by water, and how the building shuddered and shook when the grinding began, and how we dumped cob corn into the maw of the mill and how fluffy, sweet-smelling cow feed emerged a few minutes later.

I remember the miller having a fish line dangling in the millpond, hoping to hook one of the giant trout that everyone knew lived there but no one had ever seen, and how sweet the water tasted from the pipe that was tapped into a free-flowing spring near the mill dam.

I remember the county fair, with its Ferris wheel and merry-go-round, and the aroma of fried onions mixing with animal smells from the cattle barns. I recall the yell of the carnival hawkers, "Three balls for a quarter," "Ring the post and win a stuffed animal," "Knock over the milk bottles and take home a genuine Indian relic" (Made in Japan).

I remember how proud I felt when my 4-H calf won a blue ribbon, and how proud, too, was my father who helped me lead my little holstein heifer back to the cattle barn from the show ring.

I remember harness horses—pacers and trotters, that pulled little buggies with bicycle tires around the dusty racetrack, and the day when something frightened one of the horses and it reared up, slipped and sat down on the buggy, blowing out both of the tires and ending the race for the driver that day.

I remember the bright red, two-winged, two-seater, open airplane that gave half-hour rides for 50 cents, on the improvised landing strip out back of the horse barn on the far side of the racetrack. The plane roared as it bumped along the cow pasture landing strip, and lifted into the air not a minute too soon in order to climb over the row of oak trees that bordered the field.

I remember gravel country roads twisting through the countryside, along little streams, through the valleys, around steep hills, and straight as a tight string when the country was flat.

I recall country roads in winter, with wind-blown snow sifting over the tops of snow-drifts, making the roads impassable as the snow accumulated.

I remember spring mud and how the milkman—destined to travel the roads in all kinds of weather—sometimes needed the assistance of our team of horses, or tractor, to pull him from the quagmire that was the road in front of our farm.

I remember clouds of summer road dust announcing a traveler on the road, maybe a salesman coming to our house, especially if the dust cloud appeared in the afternoon.

I remember my mother's disdain for dust, in any form, on any day, for it sifted into the house and gathered on the top of the dining room table, and less noticeable, on the clock shelf, along the tops of the pictures, and just about everywhere.

I remember Christmas morning, with a stack of presents under the tree that couldn't be opened until the morning milking was done. Of receiving new socks and mittens that grandmother had knitted, and a new pair of skates, the type that clamped onto the bottom of my shoes and were tightened with a key.

I remember walking a mile to the neighbor's with a small present and a freshly baked pie, because we knew that his wife had passed away and his children had grown and moved to the city, and he was there alone on Christmas day.

I remember Christmas dinner, with aunts and uncles, and cousins, and a table spread with food like I only saw when the threshing crews came.

McCORMICK-DEERING

I remember the smell and taste of fresh made bread, spread thick with butter and homemade strawberry jam.

I remember the Sears catalog that came each spring and fall, creating never-ending wishes, and eventually ending up in the little house back of the big house.

I remember the country mailman who made the rounds each day, Monday through Saturday, no matter what the weather, and how I watched for the cloud of dust on our country road at eleven each day, because that was the time he came.

I remember the party line telephone, with ten customers, each with a special ring, long and three shorts, three shorts, and so on. When the phone rang you picked up the receiver, whether it was your ring or not. It was how you kept track of news in the community, both good and bad, exciting and ordinary.

I remember Fanny, our farm dog, who ruled over the area between the house and the barn; the dooryard, farm people called this space. Fanny announced the arrival of all cars to the dooryard. City salesmen often misunderstood the dog's intentions and sometimes stayed in their cars, tooting their horns, hoping my mother would come outside. Usually she didn't; she figured if a salesman couldn't face a friendly farm dog, he wasn't much of a salesman. After a brief period of horn tooting and waiting, he usually left.

I remember how Fanny kept the chickens in the chicken yard, the area immediately around the chicken house, barking at them if they strayed, or even rolling them in the dust if she thought they needed a stronger lesson.

I remember Fanny keeping track of my little twin brothers playing in the sand hole by the barn, nudging them back if they decided to stray toward the road.

I recall, at milking time, with but one command from my father, “Get the cows, Fanny,” she trotted away, and a half hour later appeared, walking to the rear of the cow herd strung out in a line in the lane, barking occasionally, wagging her tail, proud of doing her job well.

End Note

The wisdom of the Midwest is found in the minds and hearts of the people who live there. Wisdom is expressed in the stories people tell of earlier days and earlier times. Stories of happiness and hard work. Stories of hardship and joy. As rural people tell their stories, remember them, for in these stories are the values and beliefs that have been passed on from generation to generation, and make the Midwest what is is today.